Common Core Lessons & Activities:
Life Cycles

By Carole Marsh

Published by Gallopade International, Inc.

Printed in the U.S.A. (Peachtree City, Georgia)

TABLE OF CONTENTS

G: Includes Graphic Organizer

GO: Graphic Organizer is also available 8½" x 11" online
download at www.gallopade.com/client/go
(numbers above correspond to the graphic organizer numbers online)

What Is a Life Cycle?

Read the text and answer the questions.

The life of every plant and animal follows a series of orderly changes known as the "life cycle." The life cycle describes how living things are born, grow, create new life, and finally die. The cycle is continued by new life and repeats again and again.

Take the life cycle of an oak tree as an example. An acorn falls from an oak tree. It lands in soil, where it sprouts into a young tree, called a sapling. The sapling uses water, nutrients from the soil, and energy from the sun to grow leaves and stronger branches. The sapling grows bigger and bigger until it becomes an adult oak tree. Then the adult oak tree grows seeds, called acorns. These acorns develop, mature, and fall to the ground—and the life cycle begins again. After many years, the original oak tree will grow old and die.

All life cycles follow a similar pattern, but not all plants and animals have exactly the same life cycle. Some plants and animals look similar to their parents throughout their life cycle. Others, like a butterfly or a frog, go through very distinct changes in each stage of their life cycle.

The life cycles of animals and plants can be quite different. Some insects have a life cycle of only a day, while some tortoises can live to be nearly 200 years old! Humans have their own interesting and unique life cycles too!

1. A. Define cycle as it is used in the text.
   B. What can you infer about the term "life cycle" from its name?
2. According to the text, how does the life cycle continue?
3. How are all life cycles similar? How are they different?
4. A. Use the text to identify the stages of the oak tree's life cycle.
   B. In which part of the tree's life cycle does it create new life?
   C. Draw and label each stage.
5. Does the life cycle end when a tree dies? Cite evidence from the text to support your response.

RESEARCH & WRITING

Simple Life Cycles

Mammals, fish, birds, and reptiles have a simple life cycle. A simple life cycle has three steps: before birth, young, and adult. In a simple life cycle, the young animal looks similar to the grown adult.

Complete the research and writing prompts.

STEP 1: Choose an animal type: mammal, fish, bird, or reptile. Research the simple life cycle of the animal type you chose. Take notes and answer the following questions as part of your research.

1. How is this animal type usually born?
2. How does this animal type change from young to adult?
3. How are the adults similar to the young?
4. How are the adults different from the young?
5. What words name and describe this type of animal's life cycle?
6. What words name and describe the important events in this type of animal's life cycle?
7. What are three specific examples of this type of animal?

STEP 2: Use your research notes to complete the graphic organizer with information about the three stages of the animal type's simple life cycle.

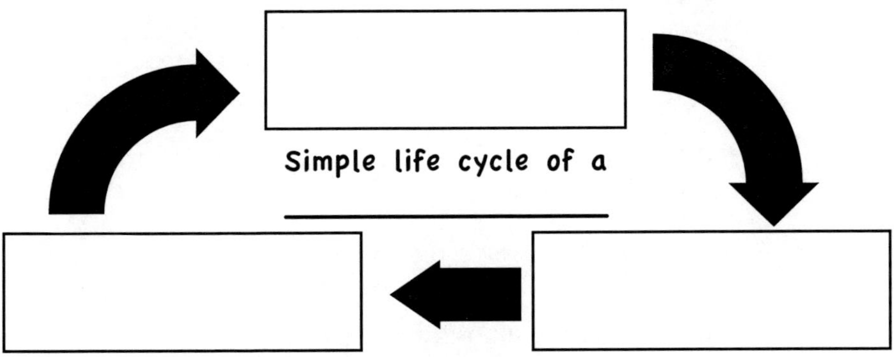

STEP 3: Create a short visual presentation about the animal type you researched. Use a combination of text and visuals to answer the questions above. Include a visual representation of the three stages of the animal type's simple life cycle. Share a few interesting facts.

STEP 4: As a class, compare and contrast the similarities and differences of the simple life cycles for mammals, fish, birds, and reptiles.

Metamorphosis

Read the text and answer the questions.

Metamorphosis is a significant change in an animal's form or structure that occurs as the animal goes from one stage to the next in its life cycle. Metamorphosis is often so significant that it results in a change to the animal's habitat or behavior.

Amphibians are a specific kind of animal. Examples of amphibians include frogs and salamanders. One of the traits of amphibians is they have a backbone. Another of their traits is they begin their life breathing water but they grow up to breathe air as an adult! How do amphibians make this change? They do it through the process of metamorphosis!

Frogs are amphibians. Frogs go through metamorphosis.

Here is a description of many of the changes frogs go through during their life:

- A frog begins its life cycle by hatching from an egg.
- A young frog can breathe water and is called a tadpole.
- A tadpole breathes water through gills on the sides of its head.
- A tadpole has a tail to help it swim.
- When a tadpole transforms into an adult frog, it undergoes these changes:
    - It grows four legs.
    - Its tail shrinks and disappears.
    - Its gills close when it develops lungs.
- A frog that breathes air and has legs is in the adult stage.
- An adult frog reproduces by laying eggs.

1. A. Use the text to write a definition of metamorphosis.
   B. Use a dictionary to write a definition of the word change.
   C. How are the meanings of these two words similar?
   D. How are the meanings of these two words different?
2. List two characteristics typical of amphibians.
3. Use the text to identify the characteristics of each stage of a frog's life cycle and record this information in the table.

Stage	**Characteristics**
Egg	
Tadpole	
Adult Frog	

4. Between which two stages does metamorphosis occur? Explain.
5. Metamorphosis often results in a change in the animal's habitat or behavior. Use the frog life cycle to explain why this occurs.

Complete Metamorphosis

Look at the photographs and text in the chart. Describe each photograph to complete the chart. Then answer the questions.

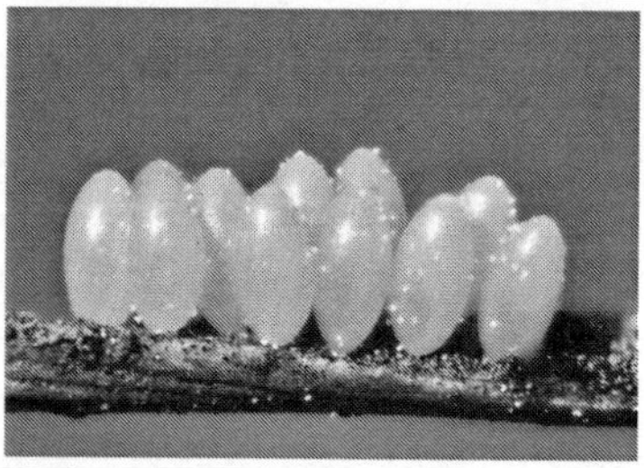	Ladybugs lay their eggs on the underside of a leaf. This is the first stage of the life cycle. **Describe it!**
	In the second stage, an egg hatches into a larva. The larva's primary purpose is to eat. It gains nutrients and energy to grow much larger. **Describe it!**
	In the third stage of the ladybug's life cycle, the larva builds a pupa around itself. During this special time, the insect transforms, even though it can't eat or move. **Describe it!**
	Lastly, the ladybug comes out of the pupa as a fully-grown adult. This is the bright red insect with black spots we see flying around our gardens! **Describe it!**

1. A. Write the name of each stage in the ladybug's life cycle on the diagram.
   B. Write a name or description of the activity that occurs between the stages beside each arrow.
   C. Circle the stage that represents complete metamorphosis.

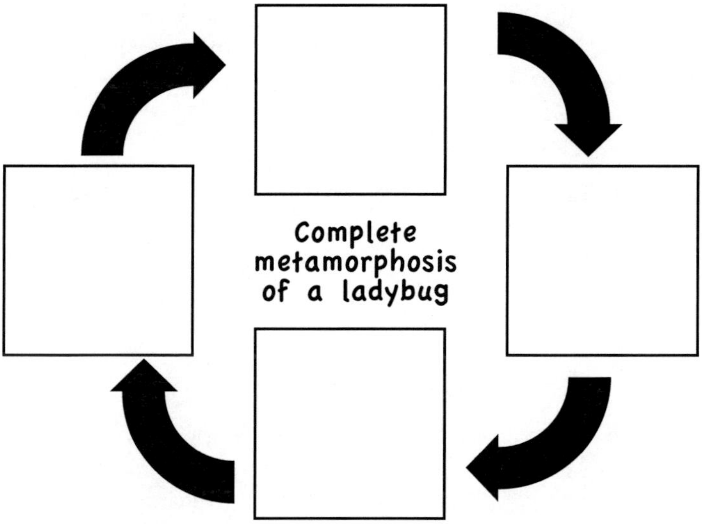

2. _____ True or False?
   An adult ladybug looks exactly like its larval shape, only larger.

3. _____ True or False?
   The larva prepares for the pupa stage by remaining still.

4. Using the chart, write which stage of a butterfly's complete metamorphosis is being described in each statement below:
   A. "Change takes a lot of energy. As a caterpillar, I eat and eat until I can't eat any more!"
   B. "I haven't been born yet! I am still waiting to hatch."
   C. "I am no longer a worm-like creature. Now I can fly, and people think I look beautiful."
   D. "I have a hard outer case. Hopefully this will protect me while I change my appearance."

5. Metamorphosis means "to transform or change shape." Explain why the process a butterfly goes through is called a metamorphosis. Make inferences from the photographs to support your explanation.

6. Research the terms, "pupa," "cocoon," and "chrysalis." Explain how the meanings of these words are similar and how they are different.

Incomplete Metamorphosis

Read the text and answer the questions.

Some insects (about 10%) go through a version of metamorphosis known as an incomplete metamorphosis. Unlike animals that go through a complete metamorphosis, which have four stages in their life cycle, animals that go through incomplete metamorphosis only have three life cycle stages.

An incomplete metamorphosis life cycle begins with an egg. The egg hatches into a <u>nymph</u>. This is the larval stage of its life cycle. A nymph has characteristics that are very different from those it will have when it is an adult. However, the nymph will not go through a pupa stage of transformation. Instead, the nymph changes slowly as it grows. At the end of the larval stage, the fully-grown adult will look remarkably different than it did at the start.

A good example of incomplete metamorphosis is found in the life cycle of a dragonfly. Dragonfly eggs are laid underwater in marshes or ponds. After the eggs hatch, the dragonfly nymphs continue to live in the water because they do not breathe air or have wings. The nymph stage may last up to 4-6 years. When the nymph is ready for metamorphosis, it climbs out of the water onto a plant. Exposure to the air allows it to start breathing. It sheds its skin and comes out as an adult dragonfly with wings. As an adult, the dragonfly can fly, live on land, and lay eggs. Adult dragonflies only live about 2 months.

1. Complete the graphic organizer about incomplete metamorphosis: Write the name of each stage in a box. Describe the process that occurs between stages on the arrows. Identify metamorphosis.

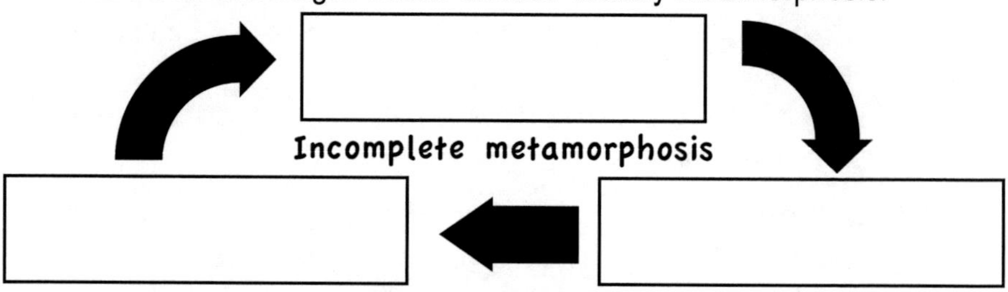

2. A. List three ways the nymph is different from the adult dragonfly.
   B. When do these changes occur? Explain your answer.
   C. How is a dragonfly's life affected by its life cycle? Explain.

Metamorphosis Types

Complete the graphic organizer by comparing and contrasting the characteristics of complete metamorphosis and incomplete metamorphosis.

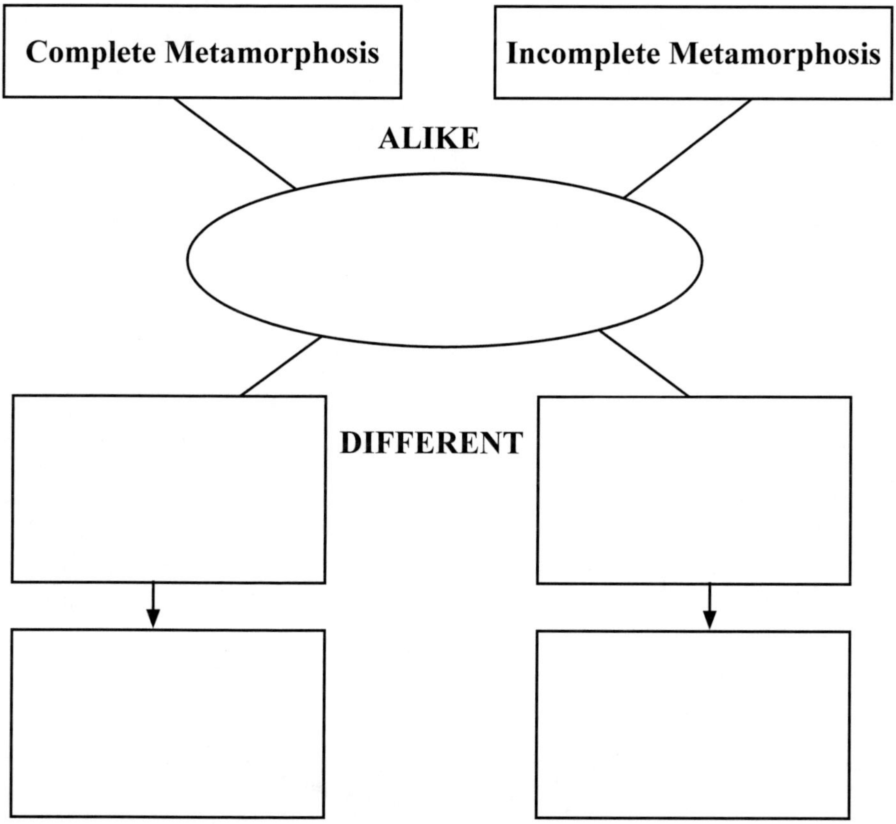

Use information from the graphic organizer to determine which type of metamorphosis is being described: complete or incomplete.

1. _____________The young larva eats and eats, preparing for the period of change. In this case, the larva looks completely different from the adult it will become.

2. _____________As a young larva changes into an adult, it changes dramatically, but not all at once. The adult is sometimes similar to the larva, usually with remarkable differences such as wings.

Simple vs. Metamorphic Life Cycles

Complete the graphic organizer by comparing and contrasting the simple life cycle and the metamorphic life cycle.

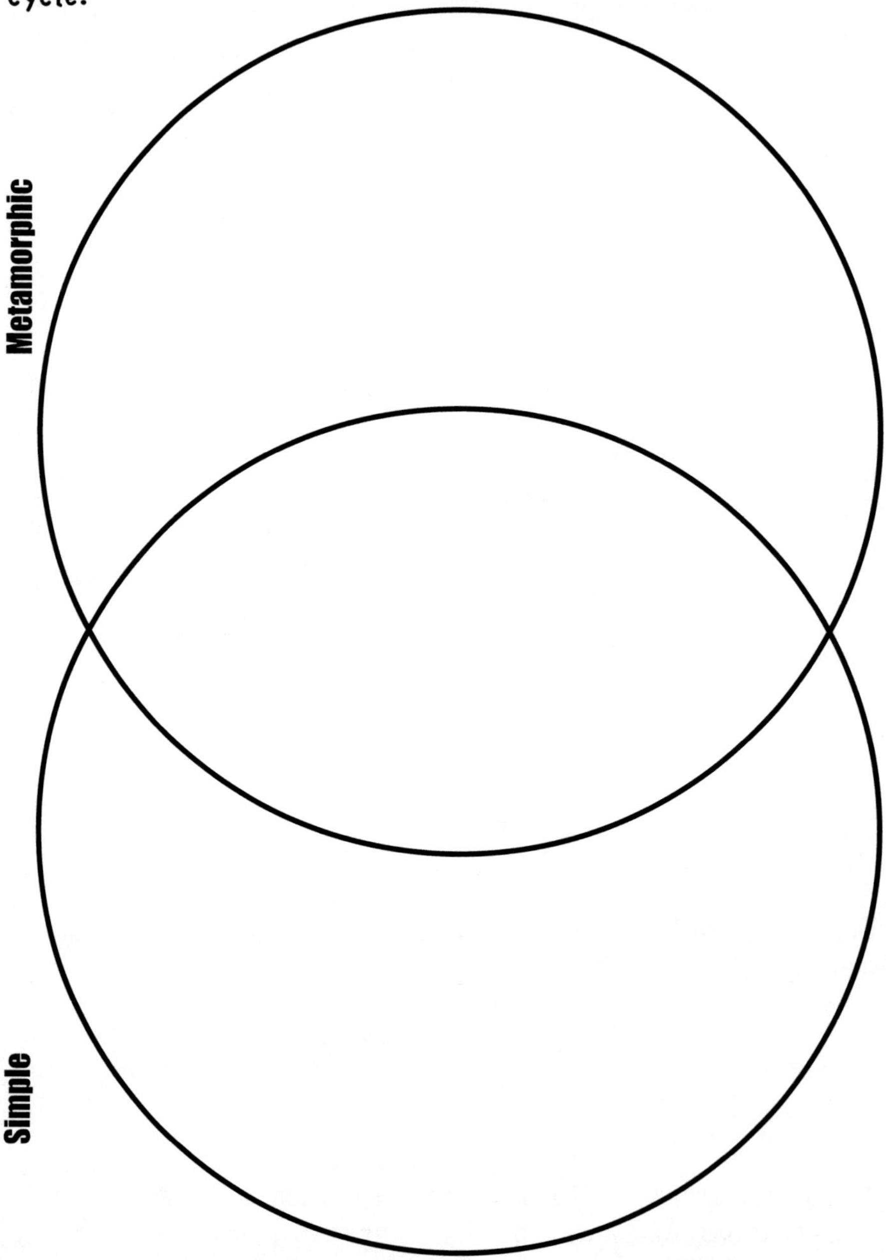

The Life of a Butterfly

The life cycle of a butterfly is often used as a symbol, simile, or metaphor for comparison with human life. Complete the chart and answer the questions.

Quotations:	The message or moral of each quotation:
"'Just living is not enough,' said the butterfly, 'one must have sunshine, freedom, and a little flower.'" — *Hans Christian Anderson*	
"We delight in the beauty of the butterfly, but rarely admit the changes it has gone through to achieve that beauty." — *Unknown*	
"There is nothing in a caterpillar that tells you it's going to be a butterfly." — *Richard Buckminster Fuller*	
"We are like butterflies who flutter for a day and think it is forever." — *Carl Sagan*	

1. Which quotation most likely comes from an author's work of fiction? Give evidence to support your choice.
2. The saying, "Don't judge a book by its cover," shares a common message with which quotation? What is the meaning of this message?
3. Use an online resource to learn more about the author of the fourth quotation. How does this knowledge affect your interpretation of his message? Describe what his quotation is likely comparing.

Poetry of Plants

Read the poem and answer the questions.

The Seedling

by Paul Laurence Dunbar

1) *As a quiet little seedling*
Lay within its darksome bed,
To itself it fell a-talking,
And this is what it said:

2) *"I am not so very robust,*
But I'll do the best I can;"
And the seedling from that moment
Its work of life began.

3) *So it pushed a little leaflet*
Up into the light of day,
To examine the surroundings
And show the rest the way.

4) *The leaflet liked the prospect,*
So it called its brother, Stem;
Then two other leaflets heard it,
And quickly followed them.

5) *To be sure, the haste and hurry*
Made the seedling sweat and pant;
But almost before it knew it
It found itself a plant.

6) *The sunshine poured upon it,*
And the clouds they gave a shower;
And the little plant kept growing
Till it found itself a flower.

7) *Little folks, be like the seedling,*
Always do the best you can;
Every child must share life's labor
Just as well as every man.

8) *And the sun and showers will help you*
Through the lonesome, struggling hours,
Till you raise to light and beauty
Virtue's fair, unfading flowers.

PART A: Identify key elements of the poem.

1. Describe the tone of the poem.
2. What point of view does the poem express?
3. What can you infer about the age of the author of the poem? Explain.
4. A. What is the message or moral presented by the poem?
   B. Who is the intended audience of this poem? Which stanzas helped to identify the audience?
5. How is the life cycle of a seedling similar to a child's life cycle? How is it different? Use your own experiences and evidence from the poem to give examples of each.

PART B: Use the text to determine who or what is being represented. Discuss each of your answers with your class.

6. "darksome bed" [stanza 1]
7. "Its work of life" [stanza 2]
8. "sun and showers" [stanza 8]

PART C: Write the number(s) of the stanza(s) that best represent(s) each stage of a plant's life cycle.

9. ____ a seed What words helped you reach your conclusion?
10. ____ a seedling What words helped you reach your conclusion?
11. ____ an adult plant What words helped you reach your conclusion?

PART D: Writing prompts

12. A. Read the poem again. Circle all words and phrases that reveal the seedling's "work of life."
    B. Do you agree or disagree that the process of growing up is difficult? Why or why not?
13. In the poem, the author states that "sunshine" and "showers" helped the seedling to grow. Think about things that help you grow. Identify at least three things and write a well-organized essay explaining how each one helps you grow. Edit and proofread your work. Share your writing with your class and discuss.

Plant Life Cycles

Read the text and answer the questions.

Just as animals have life cycles, plants have life cycles too. Plant life cycles include three stages: seed, seedling (young plant), and plant (adult). The process begins when a seed falls onto or is placed into soil. Water, sunlight and air nourish the seed until it sprouts into a seedling. The seedling grows larger and stronger toward adulthood. As an adult, a plant is able to make its own seeds for reproduction. When an adult plant's seeds are dropped or spread, the life cycle begins again.

Did you know? Some seeds grow into plants that not only produce flowers, but they also produce fruit we can eat. One common fruit-bearing plant is an apple tree. The apples contain the seeds of the apple tree. Apples that are not eaten fall to the ground and rot. The seeds inside may produce a new apple tree.

1. What is the purpose of this text?
2. Use the text to list things plants need to grow and live.
3. What special ability do adult plants have that seedlings do not?
4. If all the apples from a tree are picked, what is the result?
5. Use the text to complete the table about plant life cycles.

Stage	Describe it	Draw it

CAUSE & EFFECT

Seeds Everywhere!

Read the text and answer the questions.

Plants spread seeds in many ways. People may plant some seeds in the ground or in a pot, but most plants do not wait for people to help. Animals, water, and wind also help spread seeds to new locations.

Some plants produce sticky seeds that can get caught in an animal's feathers, fur, or even on your clothes. These seeds can then "catch a ride" on their host to another location. Other plants, such as apples, hide their seeds inside tasty fruit that is eaten by animals. The seeds travel through the animal's digestive system and are then dropped in another place.

Wind can also help spread smaller seeds, like those found in dandelions. Any seeds with wings, hair, or feather-like parts can be carried by the wind because they are so lightweight. Once the wind has carried these seeds to a new site, they can sprout on their own and begin the life cycle all over again.

Some seeds travel on their own, shooting out of their pods and sailing through the air as far as a few feet away from their parent plant! Some seeds even float in water, along rivers and streams. Seeds do not have to be small to float—coconuts are actually very large seeds, and they can float in water.

1. A. What is the main idea of the text?
   B. How does the author of the text develop the main idea?
2. List 5 characteristics of seeds that help them travel to new locations.
3. Give a cause and effect example for how each of the following items help spread seeds:

Animals	Cause:	→	Effect:
Wind	Cause:	→	Effect:
Water	Cause:	→	Effect:

PRIMARY SOURCE ANALYSIS

In the Garden

Read the text and answer the questions.

The time has come for me to plant my garden again, and I am excited about the variety of plants I'll include this year! There will be quite an assortment of plants, bushes, and even trees this time around. I will have annuals, biennials, and perennials.

One annual my garden will contain is the marigold, a type of brightly colored flower that grows fairly low to the ground. Next, I'll have tomatoes, a fruit (sometimes referred to as a vegetable) whose vines grow quite tall. Finally, I'll include petunias, another type of annual flower that is usually a vibrant purple or pink color.

The biennials in my garden will include parsley and carrots. Carrots are delicious vegetables, and many of my friends are surprised to learn that they are actually a kind of root that grows underground. Parsley is a type of herb I like to use when I cook.

The section of my garden with perennials will have roses, daisies, chrysanthemums, and even trees. The flowering rose bushes are sure to add rich fragrance and color. Additionally, I am planning to plant fruit trees, such as crabapple and peach trees, because they grow well here and will produce some food for my family. The trees will take a long time to grow and produce fruit, but I think it will be worth the wait!

I can't wait for you to come and visit so you can see my garden for yourself!

annual [**an**-yoo-uhl] *noun*: plant that lives for only one year or season; drops its seeds before it dies

biennial [bahy-**en**-ee-uhl] *noun*: plant that lives for two years; requires two years to complete its life cycle and produces seeds the second year before it dies

perennial: [puh-**ren**-ee-uhl] *noun*: plant that can live for many years; its roots do not die in the winter; usually produces seeds every year beginning in its second year

PART A: Answer these questions about the first text.

1. What is the purpose of the first text? Explain your answer.
2. Describe the writing style of the first text.
3. What inferences can you make about the author of the first text? Cite excerpts from the text to support your answer.

PART B: Answer these questions about the second text.

4. What is the purpose of the second text? Explain your answer.
5. Describe the writing style of the second text.
6. Where would you expect to find the second text?

PART C: Use both texts to answer these questions.

7. Name two plants in the garden that have a two-year life cycle.
8. Name three plants in the garden that will only live for one year.
9. Name three plants in the garden that will bloom for many years.
10. Are the trees described in the first text annuals, biennials, or perennials?
11. What types of plants produce seeds before dying?
12. Are trees typically annual, biennial, or perennial? How do you know?

PART D: Complete the Venn diagram comparing and contrasting annuals, biennials, and perennials.

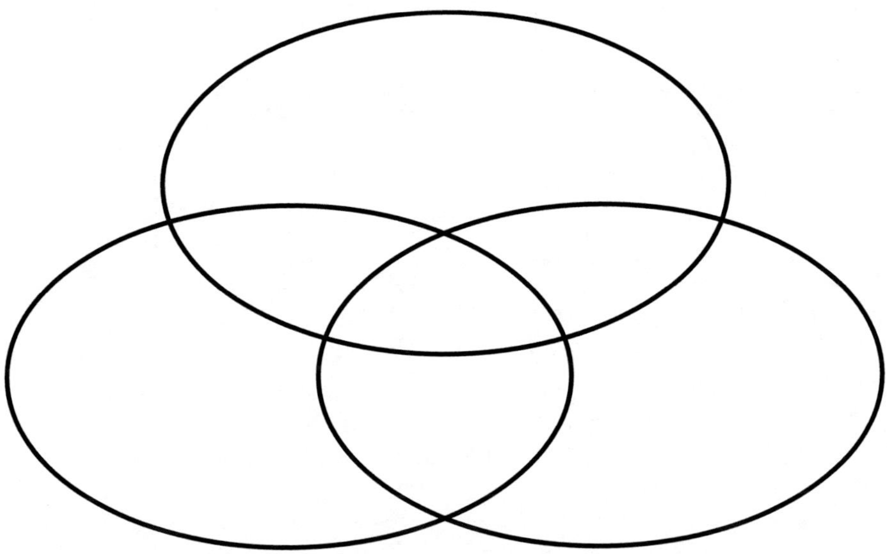

Annual, Biennial, or Perennial?

Annuals are plants that survive for only one year. Biennials are similar to annuals, except they live for two years. Perennials are plants that can live for many years.

Follow the research and writing prompts.

PART A: In small groups, take a supervised walk outside and record the names and descriptions of five plants you observe. When observing, think about how long the plant has been there and if you have seen it bloom.

Plant Name	Observation and Description
1.	
2.	
3.	
4.	
5.	

PART B: Based on observation and knowledge, predict whether each plant is an annual, biennial, or perennial.

Prediction	Plant 1	Plant 2	Plant 3	Plant 4	Plant 5
annual, biennial, or perennial?					

PART C: Use an online resource to check your predictions. Then write a short report on the results. Explain what you observed. Tell how you classified each plant and explain why. Give your reasons for labeling each plant as annual, biennial, or perennial. Which plants did you label correctly? Which ones did you label incorrectly? What conclusions can you make? Proofread and edit your work.

Life Span and Death

Read the text and answer the questions.

The lives of all plants and animals must eventually come to an end. The end of a life is called death. Life span refers to the length of time between an animal's birth and death. Some insects may only live for a few days before dying, but some animals (and even some humans) can live to be more than 100 years old. Some plants live even longer!

Death is a part of the life cycle. However, before a plant or animal dies, it usually reproduces. In this way, even though life ends, the cycle of life continues.

ORGANISM	(Approximate) LIFE SPAN
Worker bee	1 year
Red fox	14 years
Human	70-80 years
Galapagos tortoise	190 years
Onion plant	2 years
Giant sequoia tree	3,000 years

1. What is the difference between a life span and a life cycle?
2. How does a plant or animal continue a life cycle?
3. Predict what would happen if plants and animals did not age and die. Use logical reasoning to support your prediction.
4. A. In small groups, choose one of the organisms from the chart. Use an online resource to gather facts and information about the life cycle of the organism.
   B. Use computer software to create a digital presentation including text and images. Include the type of life cycle and details on the general life span of the organism.
   C. Give your presentation to your class. As a class, compare and contrast the life spans and life cycles of different animals presented.
   D. What common themes do all life cycles share?

Endangering the Life Cycle

Read the text and answer the questions.

The life cycles of plants and animals are delicate. A life cycle can be disturbed, interrupted, or stopped completely.

What can affect a life cycle? Life cycles can be altered by two means—nature or the actions of people. Sometimes a significant natural event, like a volcanic eruption, wildfire, flood, or drought, can affect a life cycle. Human activity can also have harmful effects. People may cut down forests faster than trees can grow. Human waste and pollution sometimes poisons the land, water, and air that plants and animals need to live. In some countries, hunting has caused many animals to become endangered, or even extinct.

Sometimes plants and animals become endangered—there are so few of that plant or animal left alive, it is close to becoming extinct. When a plant or animal no longer exists, it is extinct. Once something is extinct, it is gone forever.

1. Use the text to define endangered.
2. Use the text to define extinct.
3. Describe the relationship between endangered and extinct.
4. Name four natural events that can affect life cycles.
5. A. Give three examples of ways humans can affect life cycles of plants and organisms.
   B. Are these effects positive or negative? Explain your answer.
6. What effect does pollution have on the life cycles of plants and animals?
7. Use what you have learned about life cycles to explain the double-effect of events or actions that cause plants or animals to die early.
8. Research an endangered animal. Learn what is being done to try to prevent it from becoming extinct. Describe who is involved, the efforts they are making, the problems they face, and the successes they have had. Predict whether they will succeed or fail, and cite evidence from your research to support your prediction.

Endangering the Life Cycle

Complete the graphic organizer to propose a solution for one or more of the following problems threatening animal and plant life cycles:

Pollution Over-hunting Deforestation

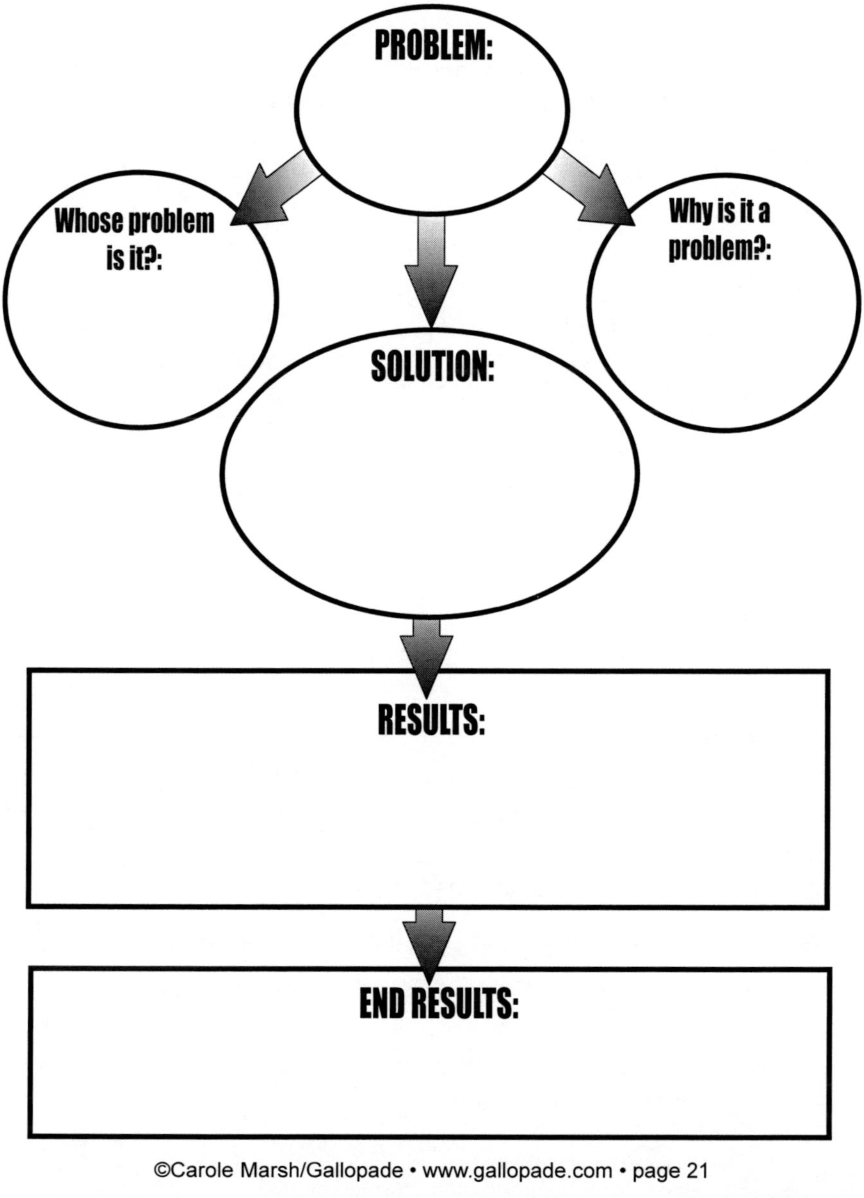

Life Cycle of a Human

Read the text and answer the questions.

Although the changes we go through in our lifetime seem significant to us, the human life cycle is considered a simple life cycle. This is because adult humans are very similar to young humans. We grow and change, but not so significantly that we don't resemble what we started as.

Many changes occur in the human life cycle. We spend our first nine months developing inside our mother. Then we are born. We grow and learn and grow. Eventually, we become adults. As adults we may reproduce, continuing the human life cycle.

Humans go through the same series as other animals who have a simple life cycle. The stages are before birth, young, and adult.

We can also divide the human life cycle into stages that represent a person's abilities and independence. When categorized in this way, we might list stages such as before birth, infancy, childhood, adolescence, and adulthood. We could divide adulthood, making separate classifications for young adults and elderly.

1. A. Use the text to create a diagram of the three-step simple life cycle of humans.
   B. Identify where you are in this life cycle.
2. A. Use the text to create a diagram of a more detailed human life cycle showing stages of independence and growth. Use your knowledge about different stages of life to describe what kinds of skills are developing and what level of independence is typical at each stage. Illustrate each stage to show what someone at that stage might look like.
   B. Identify where you are in this life cycle.
3. What role does reproduction play in the human life cycle?
4. Why is the human life cycle classified as a simple life cycle?

Life Cycle Vocabulary

Use a dictionary and other resources to complete the graphic organizer for each vocabulary word.

- annual
- biannual
- complete metamorphosis
- death
- growth
- incomplete metamorphosis
- larva
- life cycle
- life span
- metamorphosis
- nymph
- pupa
- perennial
- simple life cycle

DEFINITION	FACTS/CHARACTERISTICS
WORD	
EXAMPLES	NON-EXAMPLES

Correlations to Common Core State Standards

For your convenience, correlations are listed page-by-page, and for the entire book!

This book is correlated to the Common Core State Standards for English Language Arts grades 3-8, and to Common Core State Standards for Literacy in History, Science, & Technological Subjects grades 6-8.

Correlations are highlighted in gray.

PAGE #	READING *Includes:* RI: Reading Informational Text RST: Reading Science & Technical Subjects	WRITING *Includes:* W: Writing WHST: Writing History/Social Studies, Science, & Technical Subjects	LANGUAGE *Includes:* L: Language LF: Language Foundational Skills	SPEAKING & LISTENING *Includes:* SL: Speaking & Listening
2	RI RST . **1** **2** **3** **4** **5** 6 7 **8** 9 **10**	W WHST . 1 **2** 3 **4** 5 6 7 8 9 **10**	L LF . 1 2 3 **4** **5** **6**	SL . 1 2 3 4 5 6
3	RI RST . **1** 2 **3** **4** **5** 6 7 8 **9** **10**	W WHST . 1 **2** 3 **4** **5** **6** **7** **8** 9 **10**	L LF . 1 **2** **3** **4** 5 **6**	SL . **1** **2** 3 **4** **5** **6**
4-5	RI RST . **1** **2** **3** **4** **5** 6 7 8 9 **10**	W WHST . 1 **2** 3 **4** 5 6 7 8 9 10	L LF . 1 2 3 **4** 5 **6**	SL . 1 2 3 4 5 6
6-7	RI RST . **1** 2 **3** **4** **5** 6 **7** 8 9 **10**	W WHST . 1 **2** 3 **4** 5 6 7 8 9 10	L LF . 1 2 3 **4** **5** **6**	SL . 1 2 3 4 5 6
8	RI RST . **1** 2 **3** **4** **5** 6 7 8 9 **10**	W WHST . 1 **2** 3 **4** 5 6 7 8 9 10	L LF . 1 2 3 **4** 5 **6**	SL . 1 2 3 4 5 6
9	RI RST . **1** **2** **3** 4 **5** 6 **7** 8 9 10	W WHST . 1 **2** 3 4 5 6 7 8 9 10	L LF . 1 2 3 4 5 6	SL . 1 2 3 4 5 6
10	RI RST . **1** 2 **3** 4 **5** 6 7 8 9 **10**	W WHST . 1 **2** 3 4 5 6 7 8 9 10	L LF . 1 2 3 4 5 6	SL . 1 2 3 4 5 6
11	RI RST . **1** **2** **3** 4 **5** **6** 7 **8** **9** **10**	W WHST . **1** **2** 3 **4** 5 **6** **7** **8** **9** **10**	L LF . 1 2 3 **4** **5** **6**	SL . 1 2 3 4 5 6
12-13	RI RST . **1** **2** **3** **4** **5** **6** 7 **8** 9 **10**	W WHST . **1** **2** **3** **4** **5** 6 7 **8** 9 **10**	L LF . 1 2 **3** **4** **5** **6**	SL . **1** **2** 3 **4** 5 **6**
14	RI RST . **1** **2** **3** 4 **5** 6 7 **8** 9 **10**	W WHST . **1** **2** **3** 4 5 6 7 **8** 9 **10**	L LF . 1 2 3 4 5 6	SL . 1 2 3 4 5 6
15	RI RST . **1** **2** **3** 4 **5** 6 7 **8** 9 **10**	W WHST . 1 **2** 3 4 5 6 7 8 9 **10**	L LF . 1 2 3 4 5 6	SL . 1 2 3 4 5 6
16-17	RI RST . **1** **2** **3** **4** **5** **6** 7 **8** **9** **10**	W WHST . 1 **2** 3 **4** 5 6 7 8 9 10	L LF . 1 2 3 **4** **5** **6**	SL . 1 2 3 4 5 6
18	RI RST . 1 2 3 4 5 6 7 8 9 10	W WHST . **1** **2** 3 **4** **5** 6 **7** **8** **9** **10**	L LF . 1 **2** **3** **4** 5 **6**	SL . **1** **2** 3 **4** 5 6
19	RI RST . **1** **2** **3** **4** **5** 6 **7** 8 **9** **10**	W WHST . 1 **2** 3 **4** **5** **6** **7** **8** 9 **10**	L LF . 1 2 3 **4** 5 **6**	SL . **1** **2** 3 **4** 5 **6**
20	RI RST . **1** 2 **3** **4** **5** 6 7 **8** 9 **10**	W WHST . 1 **2** **3** **4** **5** 6 **7** 8 9 **10**	L LF . 1 2 3 **4** 5 **6**	SL . **1** 2 3 4 5 6
21	RI RST . 1 2 **3** 4 **5** 6 **7** 8 9 **10**	W WHST . 1 2 3 **4** **5** 6 7 8 9 10	L LF . 1 2 3 4 5 6	SL . 1 2 3 4 5 6
22	RI RST . **1** **2** **3** 4 **5** 6 7 **8** 9 **10**	W WHST . 1 **2** **3** **4** 5 6 **7** **8** 9 **10**	L LF . 1 2 3 4 5 **6**	SL . 1 2 3 4 5 6
23	RI RST . 1 2 3 **4** 5 6 **7** 8 9 10	W WHST . 1 2 3 4 5 6 7 8 9 10	L LF . 1 2 3 **4** 5 **6**	SL . 1 2 3 4 5 6
COMPLETE BOOK	RI RST . **1** **2** **3** **4** **5** **6** **7** **8** **9** **10**	W WHST . **1** **2** **3** **4** **5** **6** **7** **8** **9** **10**	L LF . 1 **2** **3** **4** **5** **6**	SL . **1** **2** 3 **4** **5** **6**

For the complete Common Core standard identifier, combine your grade + "." + letter code above + "." + number code above.

In addition to the correlations indicated here, the activities may be adapted or expanded to align to additional standards and to meet the diverse needs of your unique students!